THE BO

Card Games for Little Kids

by Gail MacColl

illustrations by Michael Gelen

Workman Publishing • New York

Many thanks to the hardy crew of game testers: Prudence Jarrett, Katherine Allen, Sapphire Yi-Dyer, Rose Cheeves, Al Jarrett, and Isabel Jarrett.

Copyright © 2000 by Gail MacColl and Paul Hanson

Cover and book illustrations copyright © 2000 by Michael Gelen

All rights reserved. No portion of this book may be reproduced—mechanically, electronically, or by any other means, including photocopying—without written permission of the publisher.
Published simultaneously in Canada by Thomas Allen & Son Limited.

Library of Congress Cataloging-in-Publication Data

MacColl, Gail, 1954–
Card games for little kids / by Gail MacColl / illustrations by Michael Gelen
p. cm.
ISBN: 978-0-7611-0708-8
1. Card games—Juvenile literature. 2. Family recreation—Juvenile literature. [1. Card games. 2. Games] I. Gelen, Michael, ill. II. Title.
GV1244.J37 2000
795.4—dc21

00-034974

Concept and design by Paul Hanson

Workman books are available at special discounts when purchased in bulk for premiums and sales promotions as well as for fund-raising or educational use. Special editions or book excerpts can also be created to specification. For details, contact the Special Sales Director at the address below, or send an email to specialmarkets@workman.com.

Workman Publishing Company, Inc.
225 Varick Street
New York, NY 10014-4381

workman.com

WORKMAN is a registered trademark of Workman Publishing Co., Inc.

Manufactured in China

First printing October 2000

10 9 8 7 6

CONTENTS

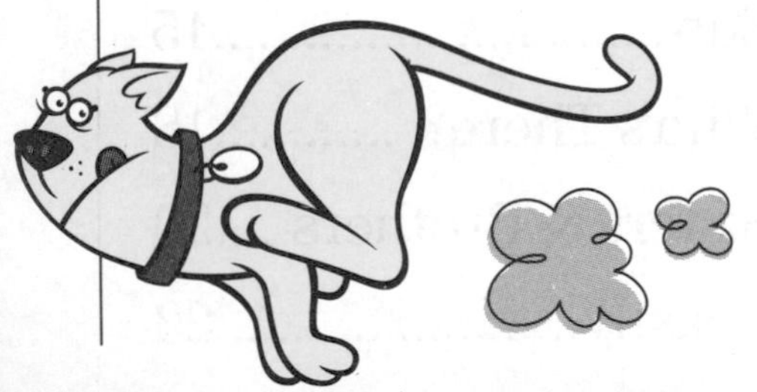

SPLASH!

WHAT'S THE DEAL?

How to have loads of fun with this book

Picture—or novelty—decks have been produced for particular card games for many years. There are specialized decks for Old Maid, Pairs, Snap, Happy Families—because kids, especially younger children, love illustrated decks. More like story books than traditional

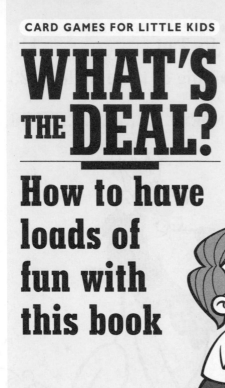

decks are, the bright colors, drawings of people or animals, and absence of numbers and symbols make them easy and fun to use. And, because picture decks have fewer cards, the card games are simpler and faster.

But you could only play one game with the usual illustrated novelty-card deck. Until, that is, *Card Games for Little Kids*. The great thing about the *Card Games for Little Kids* deck and book is that lots and lots of games—33 of them, to be exact, from the popular classics to the rare and obscure to the brand new—can be played with this one illustrated deck. The *Card Games for Little Kids* games are still quicker and easier than games with a traditional 52-card deck, but they are also full of the drama and hilarious twists and turns of luck and skill that make card-playing so enjoyable for kids of all ages.

THE DECK

NUMBER OF CARDS: 40

FAMILIES: There are 10 animal families in the deck. The families are Lion, Tiger, Zebra, Monkey, Snake, Crocodile, Giraffe, Elephant, Hippopotamus, and Rhinoceros.

FAMILY MEMBERS: Each family has four members:

Father, Mother, Sister, Brother. Fathers are always Blue, Mothers are always Red, Sisters are always Yellow, and Brothers are always Green.

SEQUENCE: The animal family order, from bottom to top, is: Brother, Sister, Mother, Father or Green, Yellow, Red, Blue.

You may have to play cards in sequence in some games and that means sticking strictly to the order.

MATCHING: Cards match when they are the same family member/same color. So two blue Father cards are a match.

SKILLS AND TIPS

SHUFFLING: You can't shuffle too much, but under-shuffling can spoil a game by distributing cards in an uneven and therefore unfair way. To shuffle: Hold the deck in the palm of your hand, as loosely as possible so that the cards are spread out a bit. Take a small chunk from the front

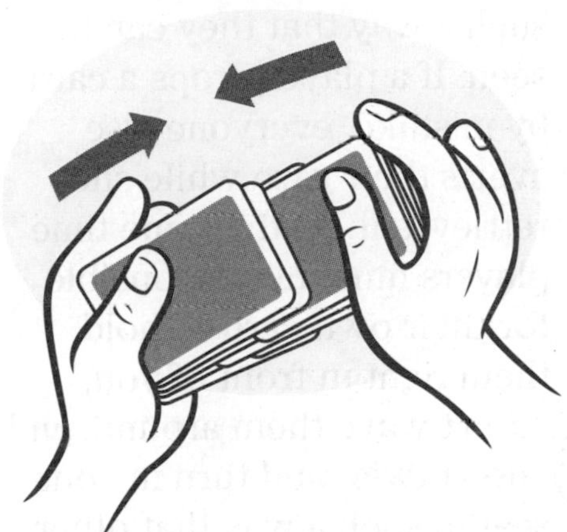

and carefully disperse the chunk in among the rest of the cards in your hand—so that the cards get as mixed up as possible. Do this several times. A simpler way is to spread the cards out, mess them around a bit, and re-collect them as randomly as possible.

DEALING: There are lots of fun ways to decide who deals—various ways are suggested throughout, but feel free to invent your own. Young children may need a lot of supervision and help with choosing a dealer and dealing. Dealing should always be done with the deck held picture-side-down. The other players must wait until the deal is finished to even touch their cards. It is very bad card manners to start picking up your cards while the dealer is still handing them out.

PEEKING: Don't look at other people's cards. Children with really excellent card manners tell another player when he or she is holding cards in such a way that they can be seen. If a player drops a card by mistake, everyone else averts their gaze while she retrieves it. At the same time players must be responsible for their own cards—hold them right in front of you, don't wave them around, and don't twist and turn in your seat in such a way that other players can't help but see what cards you have.

CHANGE-UPS: For added fun, there are suggestions at the end of some games for ways to make the game harder, easier, faster, slower, or just a bit different. Give them all a try.

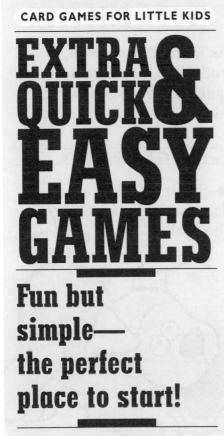

EXTRA QUICK & EASY GAMES

Fun but simple—the perfect place to start!

This section contains games designed for short attention spans and even shorter tempers. Quick-playing as well as simple, they introduce fundamental card game skills—matching, collecting, passing, discarding, dealing—in easy-to-learn, fun-to-play formats. Also introduced are the social conventions of card playing: sitting in a circle, taking turns—usually in a clockwise order—fair play, and politeness. The first games in the section are the easiest and most basic—the perfect place for absolute beginners to try out their new picture-card deck.

YAPPY

2 PLAYERS

Matching made easy—the perfect starter game for little ones and other beginners.

YOUR MISSION

As in traditional Snap, to collect all the cards by being quick to notice cards that match.

GET READY

- Sit facing each other. The younger player is the dealer.

• Players will be trying to match cards. Remember: Two family members (two Mothers, for instance) are a match.

GET SET

DEALER: Split the deck in half—it doesn't have to be exact. Keep one half of the cards for yourself and give the other half to the other player.

BOTH PLAYERS: Put your half of the deck picture-side-down in front of you.

GO!

OTHER PLAYER: You go first. Turn over the top card from your stack. Put it picture-side-up between you on the floor or table to create a center pile.

DEALER: Now you do the same, putting your card on top of the other player's card.

BOTH PLAYERS: Take turns quickly turning over the top card from your stack and putting it in the middle. When the card that one of you turns over matches the top card on the center pile, bark "Ruff! Ruff! Ruff!" loudly.

- The player who barks first gets to take the center pile. Turn the cards over so that they are picture-side-down, then add them to the bottom of your stack. Put a new card picture-side-up in the center.

- If anyone barks by mistake, the other player gets the stack of cards in the middle.

WINNER: The player who collects all of the animal cards wins.

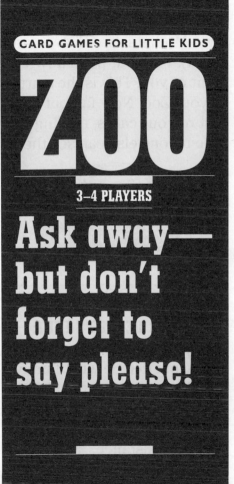

CARD GAMES FOR LITTLE KIDS

ZOO

3–4 PLAYERS

Ask away—but don't forget to say please!

YOUR MISSION

To collect the most matching pairs.

GET READY

● The smallest player is the dealer.

GET SET

DEALER: Give out all the cards one at a time and picture-side-down. Don't worry if some players have more cards than others.

EVERYONE: Pick up your cards. Look through your cards and take out any matching pairs—that is, two of any family member

(two Mothers, two Sisters, and so on). Put your pairs down in front of you. This is the start of your Zoo. Now fan out the rest of your cards, making sure no one else can see them.

GO!

PLAYER ON DEALER'S LEFT: You go first. Look at your cards and decide what family member you need to make another matching pair. Ask any other player for what you want, for instance, "Mildred,

do you have a Mother, please?" If Mildred has the card you've asked for, she must give it to you. You can keep asking for cards as long as you're successful. Remember to say "Thank you." Your turn is over when someone doesn't have a card you've asked for.

OTHER PLAYERS: You must hand over cards if you have been asked politely for them. If you don't have any of the family member you've been asked for, say, "I'm sorry, I don't have any Sisters."

EVERYONE: Keep taking turns, with play going around to the left, until all the cards have been played.

WINNER: The player with the most animal pairs in his or her Zoo is the winner.

WHO'S THERE?

1 PLAYER

Elementary solitaire—perfect for keeping amused in a restricted space.

YOUR MISSION

To get rid of all your cards.

GET READY

- Shuffle the deck well.

GET SET

- Take the deck of cards in your hand, picture-side-down. Say "Who's there?" then deal out the cards, picture-side-up. As you do this, say (or sing!) "Brother, Sister, Mother, Father," naming one family member per card. If the family

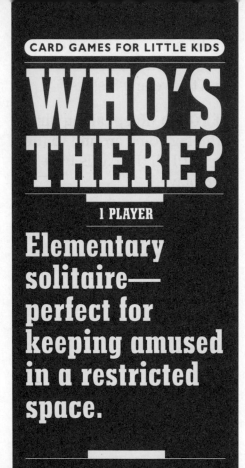

member you are naming matches the card you are turning over, remove that card from the deck.

GO!

● Just keep going. When the whole deck has been dealt, turn it over and start again. But don't lose your place in the family list. For instance, if you are on "Sister" when the deck needs turning over, then continue with "Mother."

● Eventually either all the cards will have matched your song, and been eliminated—in which case you've won—or the cards and the list keep coming around in the same order and you're stuck. In this case, you just gather all of the cards together again, reshuffle, and start over.

CARD GAMES FOR LITTLE KIDS

SISTERS & BROTHERS

5–7 PLAYERS

A real crowd pleaser: build a nice, big family!

To be the first player to collect five Brothers or five Sisters.

GET READY

- The player with the most siblings is the dealer. If it's a tie, the player with the most *younger* siblings is the dealer.

GET SET

DEALER: Shuffle the cards. Give five cards to each player, one at a time and picture-side-down. You will have some cards left over. Put these cards carefully to one side—you won't be using them again for this game.

EVERYONE: Pick up your cards so only you can see the pictures. Put all your Brothers together and all your Sisters

together. Decide which sibling you're going to try to collect, but remember—you may have to change your mind as the game goes along. Choose a card you don't want and put it picture-side-down in front of you.

GO!

EVERYONE: Slide your unwanted card picture-side-down to the player on your left, and pick up the card coming in from the player on your right.

- Put the new card into your hand and then choose another card you don't want; put it picture-side-down and slide it to the left again. Keep doing this, trying to end up with a handful of cards that is all Brothers or all Sisters.

WINNER: The first person to have cards of all one sibling shouts "Brothers!" or "Sisters!" and wins.

CHANGE-UP

ONE OF A KIND: For five players or less. Seven cards are dealt and players try to round up either an all-female hand (Mothers and Sisters) or an all-male hand (Brothers and Fathers).

CARD GAMES FOR LITTLE KIDS

BEASTLY

2–4 PLAYERS

Dominoes and then some—simple, fast, and fun.

YOUR MISSION

To be the first player to get rid of all your cards.

GET READY

● The player with the biggest feet is the dealer. All players sit in a circle.

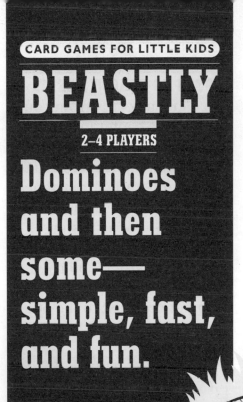

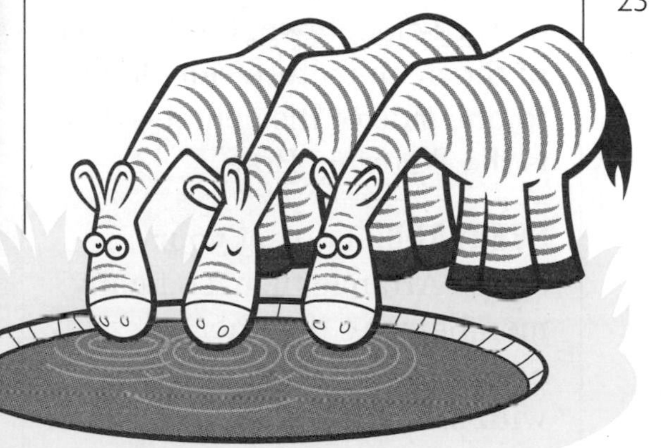

GET SET

DEALER: Turn over two cards and put them picture-side-up in the center right next to each other.

- Give out five cards to each player, one at a time and picture-side-down. Put the rest of the deck picture-side-down to one side of the center—this is the Watering Hole.

EVERYONE: Look at your cards. Arrange them so family members are together—Sisters with Sisters, Mothers with Mothers, etc.

GO!

PLAYER TO DEALER'S LEFT: You can play cards from your hand to the center in two ways—either side-by-side or end-to-end. If a center card is the Sister Giraffe for instance, and you have the same family member—another Sister card—put that out *next* to the first Sister card. If you have two Sister cards, put them both out one next to the other.

- If you have the next family member in the sequence to

one of the cards in the center—for instance the Mother Giraffe—put your Mother Giraffe above the Sister. If you have the Father as well, put him out above the Mother.

● You can build a family from the Brother cards that other players have put out, or start a new family by putting the Brother card of your choice next to any Father card.

● When you have played as many cards as you can, pick enough cards from the center to bring you back up to five. Now it's the next player's turn.

EVERYONE: Go around putting out cards and renewing your hand from the Watering Hole. Keep playing even after the Watering Hole runs dry, until someone wins or everyone runs out of cards to play.

WINNER: The first player to get rid of all his cards to the center is Beastly—and the winner.

AMAZON

2–4 PLAYERS

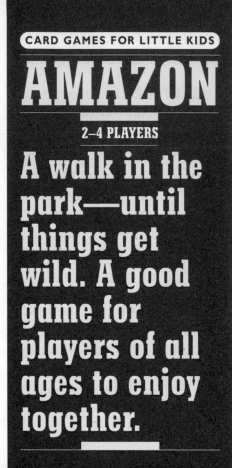

A walk in the park—until things get wild. A good game for players of all ages to enjoy together.

YOUR MISSION

To be the first player to get rid of all your cards.

GET READY

- Take turns picking cards from the deck. The first player to draw a member of the Crocodile family is the dealer.

GET SET

DEALER: Shuffle the cards. Hand out four cards to each player, one at a time and picture-side-down.

- Put the rest of the cards picture-side-down in the center. This is the Amazon. Turn up the top card and put it picture-side-up next to the Amazon.

EVERYONE: Pick up your cards. Arrange them so that all of the Fathers are on the left, Mothers next, then Sisters, then Brothers.

GO!

PLAYER ON DEALER'S LEFT: Choose any card from your hand that is either the same family member as the turned-up card or the same animal—for instance, if the top card is Mother Monkey, you can cover it with either another Monkey or another Mother. Put the card you have chosen on top of the turned-up card next to the Amazon.

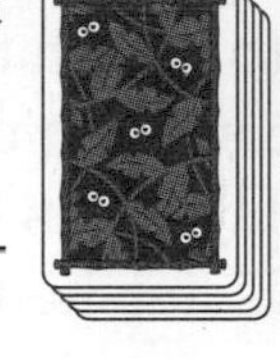

- If you can't match the turned-up card, you'll have two chances to pick a new card from the Amazon to make a match. If you haven't found a match after picking two cards, it becomes the next player's turn.

● Each player takes a turn, trying to match the top picture-side-up card. After each player has had a turn the round is finished.

PLAYER ON DEALER'S LEFT: Clear away all the picture-side-up cards and put them to one side. Turn up a new card from the Amazon and put it picture-side-up to start another round.

● Play keeps going around to the left, with a new dealer for each round.

● When the Amazon runs dry, players who can't match from their hands miss a turn.

WINNER: The first player to get rid of all her cards shouts "Amazon" and is the winner. If play is blocked—the Amazon runs dry and no one can match the center card from his hand—then the player with the fewest cards left in her hand is the winner.

CARD GAMES FOR LITTLE KIDS

GAME WARDEN

2–5 PLAYERS

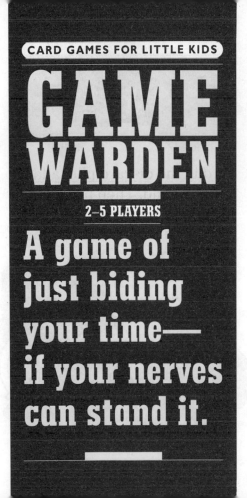

A game of just biding your time—if your nerves can stand it.

YOUR MISSION

To be the first player to round up all the members of an animal family.

GET READY

- The youngest player deals this game. Everyone sits in a circle—the game reserve.

GET SET

DEALER: Shuffle the deck well. Hand out six cards to each player, one at a time and picture-side-down.

- Put the rest of the stack picture-side-down in the center.
- Turn up the top card and put it picture-side-up next to the stack as a discard pile.

EVERYONE: Pick up your cards. Arrange them into families in your hand.

GO!

PLAYER ON DEALER'S LEFT: If you want the picture-side-up card in the discard pile, add it to your hand. Then put a card from your hand into the discard pile. If you don't want the picture-side-up card, pick a card from the stack and

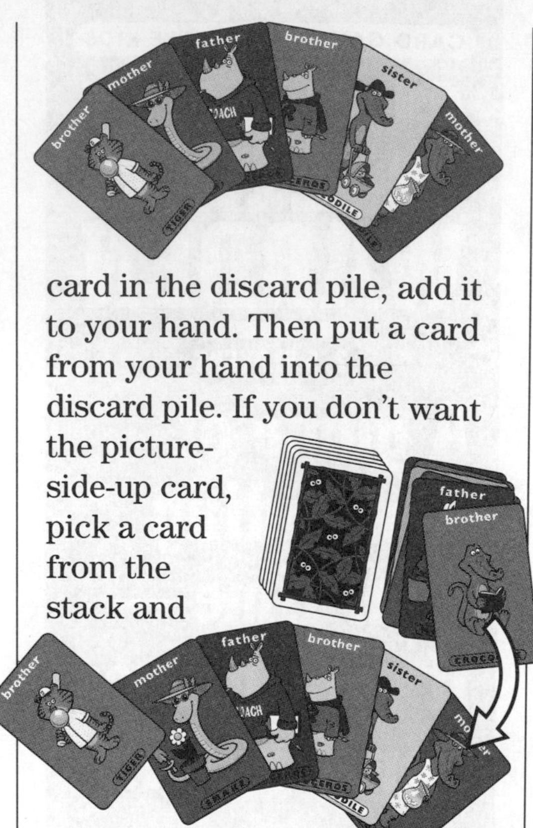

discard one from your hand. Your turn is over.

● Go around the game reserve to the left until each player has had a turn.

EVERYONE: Look at your cards. Choose one to give away. When everyone is ready, slide the card you have chosen to the player on your left.

● Keep going around, taking turns. At the end of each round, stop and slide a card to your neighbor.

● When the picture-side-down stack runs out, take the top card off the picture-side-up pile and shuffle the other cards to create a new stack.

WINNER: The first player to collect an entire family shouts "Serengeti!" then shows his family to the other players.

32

CARD GAMES FOR LITTLE KIDS

RAVENOUS RHINOS

2–5 PLAYERS

Eat or be eaten!

YOUR MISSION

To win all the cards.

GET READY

● The player with the shortest name—middle and last names included—is the dealer in this game.

GET SET

DEALER: Shuffle the cards. Give out all the cards, one at a time and picture-side-down. Don't worry if some players have more cards than others.

EVERYONE: Don't look at your cards. Keep them in a nice, neat pile in front of you.

GO!

PLAYER ON DEALER'S LEFT: You go first. Take the top card from your pile and put it picture-side-up in the center.

● Play continues around to the left, with each player turning up a card and putting it picture-side-up in the center. When someone turns up a member of the Rhinoceros family, play stops while she demands that the player sitting on her left "feed" her with picture-side-up cards, one at a time as follows: Father Rhino is fed four cards, Mother Rhino three cards,

Sister Rhino two cards, and Brother Rhino one card.

● If the player doing the feeding turns up one of the Rhino family in the process, he stops feeding and demands to be fed by the player sitting to *his* left. If that player also turns up a Rhino, then she can demand feeding from the player on *her* left and so on.

● The original Rhino player also "eats" the entire center pile and adds it to her own pile. She turns up a new card from the top of her pile and puts it in the center to resume play.

● If you lose all your cards, you are out of the game.

WINNER: The player who eats all (or most) of the cards is the winner.

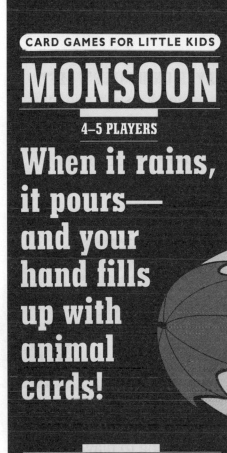

CARD GAMES FOR LITTLE KIDS

MONSOON

4–5 PLAYERS

When it rains, it pours—and your hand fills up with animal cards!

YOUR MISSION

To be the first player to get rid of all your cards.

GET READY

● The animal that really loves a good thunderstorm is the hippopotamus, so the first

player to pick a Hippo card can be the dealer.

GET SET

DEALER: If there are only four players, remove one animal family from the deck. For five players, use the entire deck. Shuffle the cards and hand them all out, one at a time and picture-side-down.

EVERYONE: Pick up your cards and arrange them in your hand. Put the same family members together in one section (so that, for instance, all the Mothers are next to each other).

GO!

PLAYER ON DEALER'S LEFT: Start the Monsoon pile by playing a card into the center. Play the family member you have most of—if you have a lot of Sisters, play a Sister.

EVERYONE: Play then goes around clockwise, with each player trying to play Sisters or whatever family member was put out by the first player. If you do not have any of that family member in your hand, you must add all the Monsoon cards to your hand.

● The Monsoon victim starts a new round by putting out a card to start another Monsoon pile—you may not play the same family member you just collected so many of.

● When each player has had a turn, the round is over. If the monsoon pile has not rained into someone's hand, it is collected and put to one side.

● The person sitting next to the player who started the last round puts out any card of her choosing to start the next round.

WINNER: The first person to play his last card is the winner.

ROAR!

3–4 PLAYERS

A game for talented animal noise-makers.

YOUR MISSION

To get rid of all your cards while purring, growling, and roaring—in that order.

GET READY

● Take turns picking cards from the deck and putting them picture-side-up. The first player to pick a member of the Lion family is the dealer.

GET SET

DEALER: Make sure all the cards are well shuffled. Hand them all out, one at a time and picture-side-down. Don't worry if some players have more cards than others.

EVERYONE: Pick up your cards. Organize the cards in your hand so that the families are together.

GO!

PLAYER ON DEALER'S RIGHT: Put a card picture-side-up in the center.

NEXT PLAYER: You have to play another member of the

same family. Put your matching card next to the first card and purr gently like a newborn cub.

● If you can't play the same family, say "Pass."

● The next player to put out a member of the same family places it beside the first two, then growls ominously like a protective lioness.

● If you play the fourth family member, roar like a fighting lion, then start another round by putting out a member of another animal family.

● If you have two or three of the same family, put them out at the same time, with the appropriate noise. So if the player before you purred, then you play your two cards followed by a growl, then a roar.

WINNER: The first player to get rid of all her cards wins.

I GUESS

2–6 PLAYERS

All you need is luck—or powers of extrasensory perception. Betting for beginners.

YOUR MISSION:

To win as many treats as possible by guessing what card will be turned up next.

GET READY

You'll need a lot of floor space or a very big table for this

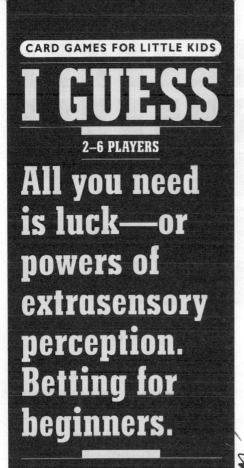

game. You'll also need a packet of M&M's or other treats. The player with an "L"—for Lady Luck—in his first name is the dealer. If no one's name has an "L," then whoever has a letter closest to "L" in her first name is the dealer.

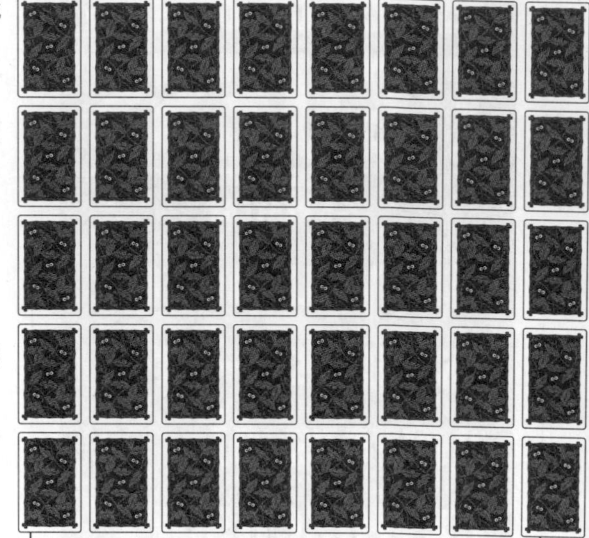

GET SET

DEALER: Shuffle the deck well. Lay out all the cards picture-side-down in a big rectangle.

EVERYONE: Say what card—Sister Tiger for instance—you guess will be the last card to be turned over. Remember your guess—you'll need it again at the end of the game.

GO!

PLAYER TO DEALER'S LEFT: Point to a card—any card—and say "I guess . . . " and say what card you think it might be, for instance "Brother Crocodile."

DEALER: Turn over the card. If the player was right he gets two M&M's. If he was half right—for instance it was a Brother but not in the Crocodile family—he gets one M&M. Leave the card picture-side-up.

● Keep taking turns going around in a circle, guessing and turning over cards. As you go along you should begin to know what *not* to guess, because certain cards will have been turned over.

EVERYONE: When only one card remains, play stops. Remember the guesses you made about what the last card would be? If, by some extraordinary piece of luck, someone guessed right, then she gets ten M&M's.

WINNER: The player with the most M&M's is the winner.

OLD FAVORITES

Oldies-but-goodies, served up fresh!

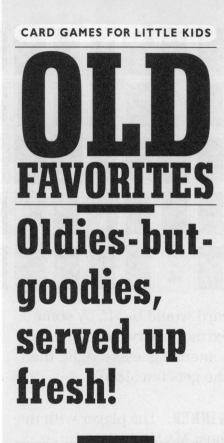

This section features animal-card versions of the most popular and well-loved card games for children. These are the games all self-respecting players must have in their card game arsenal. They're simple enough to be played well by all children, but with enough challenge to entice grown-ups—whom the children then soundly beat. Perfect family fare.

CARD GAMES FOR LITTLE KIDS

WOOF

2–4 PLAYERS

Animal Snap. You'll need extra-sharp eyes and a nice loud bark to win.

YOUR MISSION

To win as many cards as possible by noticing matching cards before anyone else does.

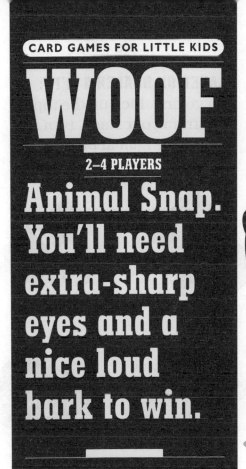

GET READY

EVERYONE: Sit in a circle. The oldest player is the dealer.

GET SET

DEALER: Shuffle the cards. Hold the deck picture-side-down. Give a card to each person, including yourself, one at a time around the circle until all the cards have been handed out. It doesn't matter if some players have more cards than others do.

EVERYONE: Put all your cards, picture-side-down, in a nice, neat stack in front of you, but don't look at them.

GO!

PLAYER ON DEALER'S LEFT: You go first. Pick up the top card from your stack, turn it over so the animal picture shows, and put it down next to your stack.

EVERYONE: Take turns going clockwise around the circle, each player turning up a picture card. Start watching for cards that are the same family member—Sister Zebra matches Sister Snake, for example.

● When you see two cards that match—and one doesn't have to be on your stack—bark "Woof!" The first player to bark wins the piles of cards under the two matching cards. Put your new cards picture-side-down at the bottom of your stack. Turn up the next card from the top of your stack.

● If you run out of cards, turn over your picture-side-up pile and use it again.

● If you bark by mistake, give each of the other players a card from your picture-side-down stack.

● If two players bark at the same time, put their piles with the matching cards on top in the middle of the circle. This is the Snap Zoo. The first person to turn up a card with the same family member as the Snap Zoo cards wins the entire Zoo. Add the Zoo cards to your picture-side-down stack.

● If you lose all your animal cards, you're out of the game.

WINNER: The winner is the first player to collect all of the cards.

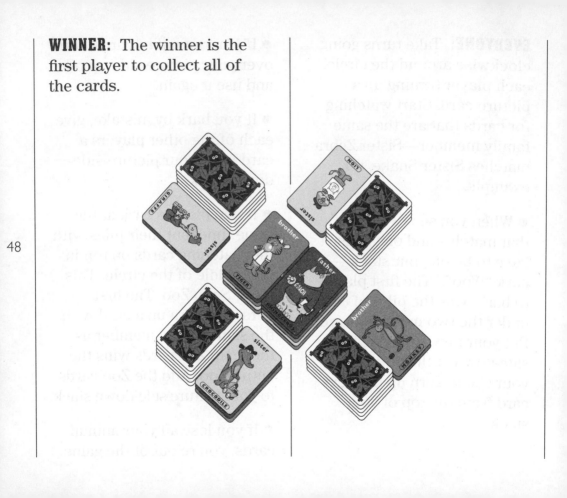

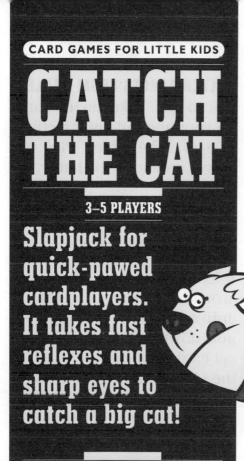

CARD GAMES FOR LITTLE KIDS

CATCH THE CAT

3–5 PLAYERS

Slapjack for quick-pawed cardplayers. It takes fast reflexes and sharp eyes to catch a big cat!

YOUR MISSION

To win all the cards by being the first player to spot Lion or Tiger cards being played.

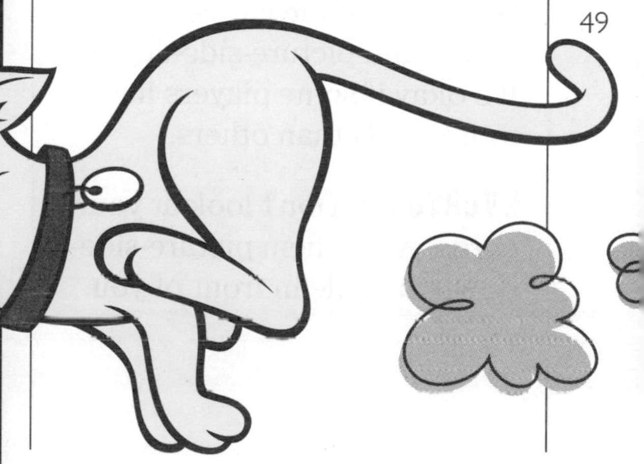

GET READY

● Sit in a circle. Everyone takes turns growling like a big cat in the jungle—the best growler gets to be the dealer.

GET SET

DEALER: Shuffle the cards. Hand out all the cards, one at a time and picture-side-down. It's okay if some players have more cards than others.

EVERYONE: Don't look at your cards. Keep them picture-side-down in a pile in front of you.

GO!

PLAYER ACROSS FROM DEALER: You go first. Take the top card off your pile and put it picture-side-up in the center. Play moves around to the left.

NEXT PLAYER: Put your top card picture-side-up on top of the card just played.

● Keep going around the circle until someone puts down a big cat card—one of the Lion or Tiger family. As soon as you see the big cat, slap your little paw right down on top of it.

- If you're the first paw on the pile, you've caught the cat! Growl—and then take the whole pile of cards from the center and put it picture-side-down at the bottom of your own stack.

- The next player in the circle starts off a new center pile by putting out a card, picture-side-up, from the top of his stack.

- If you lose all your cards, you can still try to stay in the game: Just stay beady eyed and catch the very next cat. Then you can take the whole pile of cards from the center, turn it picture-side-down, and play on. Otherwise, you're out.

- If you accidentally catch a card that isn't a cat, you must give one card to each of the other players.

WINNER: The winner is either the person who has won all the cards or the last player still to have cards left in her stack.

CREATURE FEATURE

2–6 PLAYERS

Just like Animal Noises: a traditional card game that's easy, fun—and really, really noisy!

YOUR MISSION

To win all the cards by making matches.

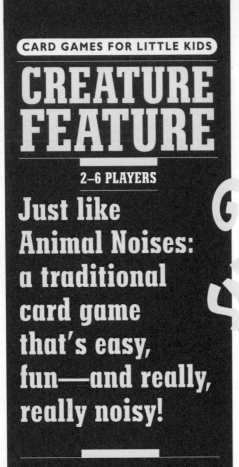

GET READY

EVERYONE: Sit in a circle. Think about feeding time at the zoo and how active and noisy the animals get at lunchtime. Look through the whole deck of cards and practice making a noise for each animal—a roar for the Lion, a hiss for the Snake, a whinny for the Zebra, a bellow for the Elephant. Add body language as well—a swinging trunk for the Elephant, claws outstretched for the Tiger, a yawn and shake of the mane for the Lion. Get everyone to agree on what sound and body movement go with which animal.

- Everyone draws a card from the deck. Whoever picks the noisiest animal is the dealer.

GET SET

DEALER: Shuffle the cards. Give them all out, one at a time and picture-side-down. Some players will have more cards than others.

EVERYONE: Don't look at your cards. Put them picture-side-down in a pile in front of you.

GO!

PLAYER ON DEALER'S LEFT: You go first. Turn over your top card and put it next to your pile picture-side-up so that everyone can see it.

EVERYONE: Moving around the circle, each player turns up a card from his or her pile.

54

- Watch closely for someone to turn over a card featuring any member of the same animal family as your picture-side-up card. This may not happen right away.

- When you spot a match, make the noise and display the body language of the matching animal family, three times in a row, really loudly. Then take the other player's entire picture-side-up pile and add it to the bottom of your own picture-side-down pile.

- If two players spot a match at the same time, the

first one to finish imitating the animal wins the pile.

- If you make the wrong noise or forget the movement, you have to give your picture-side-up pile to the player with the matching card.
- If you run out of cards, turn over your picture-side-up pile and keep playing.

WINNER: The winner is the person who has collected all the cards. The winner then deals for the next round.

CHANGE-UPS

SILENT FEATURE: To turn the volume down on this game, imitate animals without the sound—for instance, just yawn spectacularly three times when you spot a Lion match.

BUDDY SYSTEM: To make it more of a challenge, each player chooses an animal to be. When you spot a match you must imitate that player's animal, three times in a row. Hesitate, and someone else may get there first; make a mistake, and your picture-side-up pile goes to the other player.

GORILLA WAR

2 PLAYERS

There's nothing like a good old game of War, jungle-style. It's for players who are prepared to be patient and wait for the chance to pounce.

YOUR MISSION

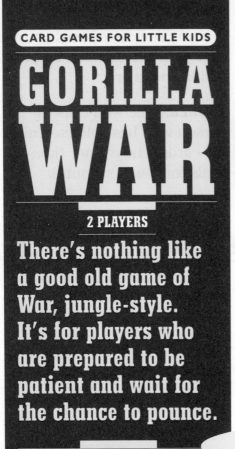

To win all the cards.

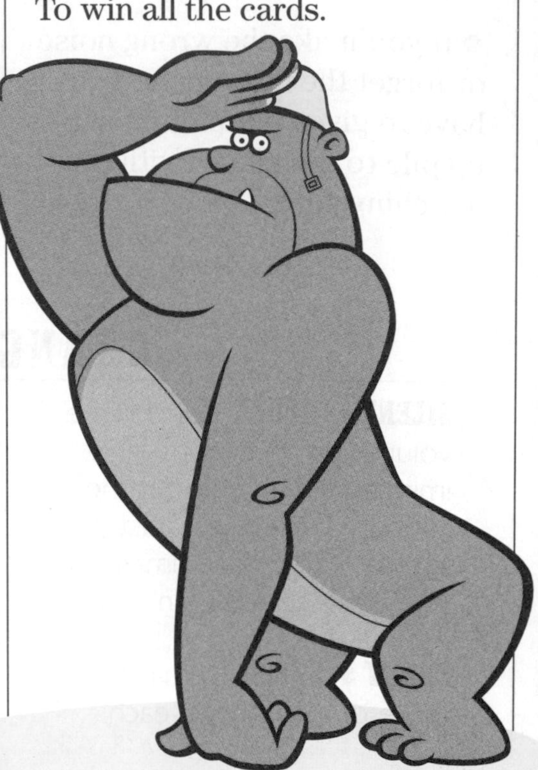

GET READY

- Warm up with some gorilla-style chest beating—and then agree to take turns dealing.

GET SET

DEALER: Shuffle the cards. Hold the deck picture-side-down and divide it in half. Give one half to the other player and keep one half for yourself.

BOTH PLAYERS: Don't look at your cards. Keep your half-deck picture-side-down in front of you.

GO!

BOTH PLAYERS: Turn over your top card and put it picture-side-up next to the other player's card in front of you. Whoever has the higher-ranking family member on his or her card picks up both cards and adds them to the bottom of her picture-side-down stack.

● Keep turning over cards at the same time and putting them in the middle next to each other, until you turn over two matching cards—two Sisters, for instance. Now it's time for Gorilla War.

BOTH PLAYERS: On top of your matching card put another card—only this one should be picture-side-down. Then turn up another card and put it picture-side-up on top of the picture-side-down card. Whoever has the highest-ranking card wins the war and adds all six cards to his stack. If your cards match again, it's Gorilla War again.

WINNER: Keep going—and this can take a while—until one player has won all the cards.

CARD GAMES FOR LITTLE KIDS

NOAH'S ARK

2–4 PLAYERS

Save the animals from the great flood, two by two, in this version of the card game classic Concentration.

YOUR MISSION

To collect the most animal pairs.

GET READY

- You'll need a lot of space on the floor or a big table. Make sure the cards are well shuffled.

GET SET

● Remember what constitutes a pair: two of the same family members (two Mothers, for instance).

● Everyone lays out all the cards together in rows, picture-side-down, in a big rectangle. Keep the cards close together but make sure they're not touching each other.

● In this game, the play goes by alphabetical order of first names.

GO!

FIRST PLAYER: Turn over any two cards so that they are

picture-side-up. Make sure all the other players have a chance to see them. Everyone is trying his or her hardest to remember those two animals and where they are before they get turned over again.

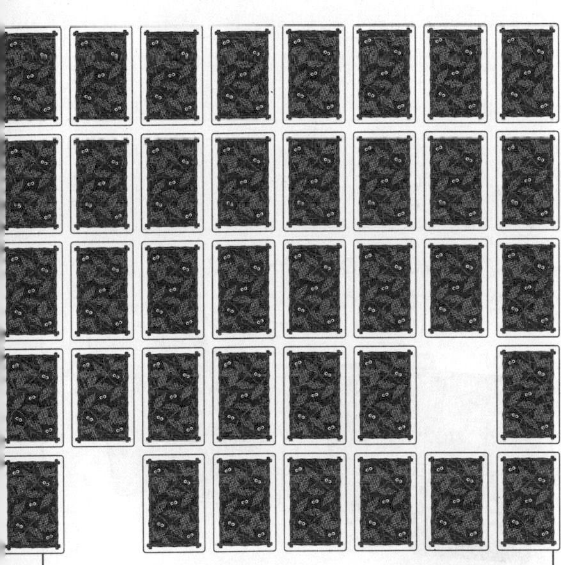

● If the two cards match, then you can take your matching pair and put them in your pile beside you. This pile is your Ark. Turn over another two cards. You can keep your turn as long as you keep turning over matching pairs.

● If the two cards don't match, turn them back over picture-side-down. It's the next player's turn now.

EVERYONE: Keep taking turns trying to find pairs to add to your Ark. Play continues until all the animals have been paired and there are no cards left.

WINNER: The player with the most animal pairs in his Ark is the winner. The winner collects all the animal pairs and shuffles them together until they're well mixed. Then everyone lays out the deck again and play starts anew.

CHANGE-UP:

TWO BY TWO: Play is exactly the same except that the pairing is more precise. You must match the Mother and Father or Brother and Sister of the same family in order to take them to your Ark. You really need to pay attention to the cards that other players turn over. Don't expect this to be a fast game!

CARD GAMES FOR LITTLE KIDS

WILD THING

2–4 PLAYERS

An element of surprise and suspense keeps players on their guard in this Crazy Eights–style game. When will the Wild Thing strike?

YOUR MISSION

To get rid of all your cards.

GET READY

- Choose an animal family to be the Wild Things. After you've decided, take turns picking a card until one player picks a member of that family; that player deals the first round.

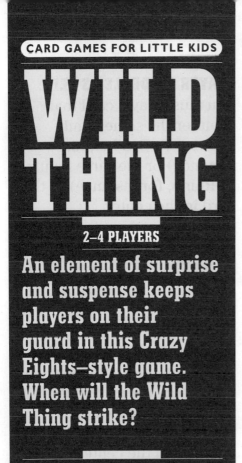

DEALER: Shuffle the cards. Hand out five cards to each player, one at a time and picture-side-down.

● Put the rest of the cards picture-side-down in a neat stack in the center. Turn over the top card and put it beside the stack. (If the top card is a Wild Thing, put it back in the middle of the stack somewhere and turn over the next card in the stack instead.)

EVERYONE: Pick up your cards and organize them so family members are together.

PLAYER ON DEALER'S LEFT: You must play a card that is either the same family member (a Brother, for instance) or the same family (a Rhino, for instance) as the card in the center.

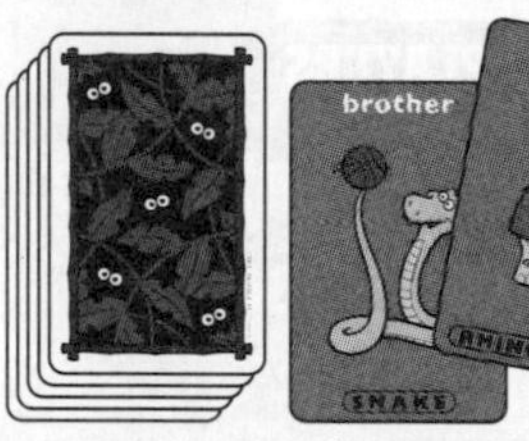

● If you don't have a card you can put in the center, you can either play a Wild Thing—but you don't have to if you'd rather save it—or start picking cards from the center stack and adding them to your hand until you pick a card that you can play.

● If you do play a Wild Thing, you must then name what family the next player must play. For instance, if Snakes are wild, you might play the Father Snake and say "Zebras" and the next player will have to play a Zebra. Try to keep track of what families have already been played. You are trying

to choose something your neighbor is unlikely to have!

● If the stack in the center runs out before you find a card you can play, take the pile of picture-side-up cards from under the top card, shuffle them well, turn them picture-side-down, and keep picking.

● Keep taking turns, going clockwise, with players trying to get rid of their cards into the center and avoid having to pick from the center stack. If the center stack runs out and no one can make a play, the round is finished.

WINNER: The first player to get rid of all his cards or to have the fewest cards when play stops is the winner.

HATARI!

2 PLAYERS

The jungle version of good old Spit. Hatari means "danger" in Swahili, so stay alert! You might have to spring into action at any moment.

YOUR MISSION

To lose all your cards.

GET READY

● Take turns picking cards from the deck. Whoever picks a Sister card gets to deal the first round—after that, take turns.

GET SET

DEALER: Shuffle the cards. Hand them out, one at a time and picture-side-down. You should each have twenty cards.

BOTH PLAYERS: You must now lay out your cards in the Hatari format. Put out four cards, the first one on the left picture-side-up, the following three picture side down. Do this again, only this time put another picture-side-up card next to the first one and on top of the first picture-side-down card. Then cover the remaining picture-side-down cards with two more picture-side-down cards. Do this two more times, so that you are faced with a row of four picture-side-up cards.

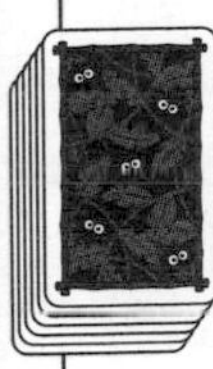

● Put your remaining cards at the left-hand end of your row of cards in a picture-side-down stack. This is your Hatari pile.

GO!

DEALER: Shout "Hatari!" to start the game.

BOTH PLAYERS: Turn over the top card from your Hatari pile and put it picture-side-up in the center.

- Try to cover the cards in the center with picture-side-up cards from the row in front of you. You can only cover a card if you have the next family member in the hierarchy sequence—so you can put a Mother on top of a Sister in the center, and the sequence goes in a circle so that a Brother can be played on top of a Father. They don't have to be from the same family.

- When you play a picture-side-up card from your row, turn over the card under it.

- You can play cards from your row onto cards that the other player has put into the center.

• When neither of you has a card you can play, you both shout "Hatari!" together and each play a card from your Hatari piles. Play on if you can; if you can't, shout "Hatari!" again, and put out more cards.

• If your Hatari pile runs out, take the top card off your center pile, leave it in the center, and take the rest of the cards from underneath. Shuffle them well and place them picture-side-down to make a new Hatari pile.

WINNER: The first player to play all of the cards from her row is the winner.

CHANGE-UP

JAMBO!: A slower, more nerve-racking version of Hatari! (Jambo means "hello" in Swahili), this game has the same setup but players take turns instead of playing cards to the center simultaneously.

• Both players draw a card before playing; the player with the higher card goes first, the player with the lower card deals.

• The dealer puts one card picture-side-up in the center.

(continued on next page)

CHANGE-UP *(continued)*

• Both players turn up the top card from their Hatari piles but don't play them to the center.

• The first player makes as many plays as he can from his row to the center card. He may use the card from his Hatari pile once to help things along, but he doesn't have to play it. (And he may not want to play it, if it is going to make things easy for his opponent.) If he plays it, he turns the next card in the Hatari pile picture-side-up.

• When the first player gets stuck, it becomes the other player's turn. His turn lasts as long as he has cards to play.

• Play continues until one player has played all the cards from his row—he is the winner.

(Note: If both players are stuck, here's one solution—have the player whose turn it isn't play a card from her Hatari pile.)

CARD GAMES FOR LITTLE KIDS

ANIMAL FAMILIES

3–6 PLAYERS

Traditionally known as Happy Families, this card game has the feel-good factor of family togetherness.

YOUR MISSION

To collect as many Animal Families as possible.

GET READY

● The player with the most letters in his or her name is the dealer. Middle names count.

GET SET

DEALER: Shuffle the cards. Give them all out, one at a time and picture-side-down. Don't worry if some players have a card or two more than others.

EVERYONE: Pick up your cards and arrange them—making sure no one else can see them—so that members of the same family are together. Think about what families you are going to try to collect.

GO!

PLAYER ON DEALER'S LEFT: You go first. Ask one of the other players—you can choose

anyone—for the exact card you want. For instance, you might say, "Stanley, do you have the Sister Monkey?" You can't ask for cards from a family you don't have in your hand. It's your turn for as long as other players have the cards you ask for.

EVERYONE: If you have the exact card you are asked for you must hand it over. If you don't have the exact card, then say so. It's your turn now.

● Keep taking turns and collecting families. When you have a complete Animal Family, put all four cards in a pile in front of you.

● If you run out of cards by making a family, you must sit out the rest of the game. If you run out in the middle of a turn, the player who gave you the last card goes next.

WINNER: When all the Animal Families have been collected, the game is over. The player with the most Animal Families is the winner.

CHANGE-UP

● To extend the game, decide beforehand that the winner is the player who has collected the most Animal Families over a certain number of deals —say, seven—or the first player to get to a certain total—for instance six families—and keep dealing and playing until that total has been reached.

VIPER

3–6 PLAYERS

A quick and fun version of Old Maid—only in this deck, it's the deadly viper that slithers venomously from hand to hand.

YOUR MISSION

To get rid of all your cards by making matching animal pairs. The player left with Father Snake is the loser.

GET READY

- Remove the Snake family from the deck—except for Father Snake. Put the rest of the Snake family to one side—they're not in this game.

- Someone who's not the oldest or the youngest can deal this game—if there are a few middles, pick the person who can do the best snake imitation.

- Everyone sits in a circle.

GET SET

DEALER: Shuffle the cards. Give them all out, one at a time and picture-side-down. Some players will have more cards than others.

EVERYONE: Look at your cards, but don't let anyone else see them.

- If you have any two animals from the same family—two Hippos, for instance—put them picture-side-down in front of you.

● If you have three matching animals, put two down and keep one in your hand.

● If you have four—the whole Giraffe family, for instance—put them all picture-side-down in front of you.

GO!

PLAYER ON DEALER'S LEFT: You go first. Fan your cards out picture-side-down in front of you so that the player on your left can choose one.

NEXT PLAYER: If the card you have chosen belongs to a family you already have, put the pair picture-side-down in front of you. If it doesn't belong to any of your families, put it in with the rest of your cards. Now spread your cards out, picture-side-down, so that the player on your left can choose one.

● Keep going around the circle. Tension mounts as the Viper slides into one player's hand and then slithers away. Try to disguise your dismay if the deadly serpent sneaks into your cards—you want to get someone else to pluck it away. Or pretend you do have the Viper and make the player sitting next to you nervous about getting bitten every time she has to choose a card from your hand.

- Players choose cards and put down animal pairs until everyone has run out of cards. Everyone, that is, except the "Viper"—the player left wrestling with Father Snake!

WINNER: There isn't a winner in this game, only a loser!

- The Viper picks up all the cards and deals the next round.

CHANGE-UP

PYTHON: A more venomous version of Viper.

- Remove only Sister Snake from the deck.
- Pairing is more difficult—only the Father and Mother or Brother and Sister of each family make a pair.
- The player left holding Brother Snake is the "Python."

SAFARI

3–5 PLAYERS

High adventure for even the littlest kids. An animal cards version of that old favorite Go Fish. Happy hunting!

YOUR MISSION

To be the first person to get rid of all the cards in your hand by making families.

GET READY

- In this game the oldest player is the dealer.
- Everyone sits in a circle.

GET SET

DEALER: Shuffle the cards. Hand them out to the other players, one at a time and picture-side-down. If you have three players, deal out five cards to each. If you have four or five players, give each player four cards.

● Make the Safari pile by putting the rest of the cards picture-side-down in the center of the circle.

HUNTERS: Pick up your cards. Make sure none of the other big game hunters can see your animals. Organize your cards so that animals from

the same family are next to each other in your hand.

GO!

HUNTER ON DEALER'S LEFT: You go first. Think about what card you need to make an animal family. Choose another player and ask for the animal you need. For instance, you might ask, "Carla, do you have any Lions?"

● If Carla has any Lions, she must give them to you. You may then ask her or another player for a different kind of animal, or ask the other player for the same animal again. You can't ask for cards from a family you don't have in your hand.

● You may keep asking as long as other players have what you are hunting for. Each time you round up all four animals in a family, put them picture-side-down in front of you.

ALL HUNTERS: If you don't have the animal family you are asked for, say "Happy hunting!" The hunter then picks a card from the Safari pile. If the card she picks is from the family she was trying to track down, she shows the card to the other players and carries on with her turn. Otherwise, she puts it in her hand and her turn is over.

● The hunt moves around the circle, with each player asking and hunting and rounding up families.

WINNER: The first one with no cards left is the winner. If two hunters run out of cards at the same time, the player with the most animal families is the Happy Hunter.

- The Happy Hunter rounds up all the cards. He is the dealer for the next game.

CHANGE-UP

BIG GAME SAFARI: A more challenging version that will slow down play and appeal to those players who have mastered ordinary Safari. The rules are the same, except that hunters must ask for a specific card: for instance, "Edward, do you have Sister Snake?" If Edward has Snakes but not the Sister he can answer, "Happy hunting!" Concentrate and try to keep track of who has asked for which cards.

JUNGLE RUMMY

2–5 PLAYERS

One of the most popular card games ever, here in a quick-and-easy animal cards version.

YOUR MISSION

To get rid of all your cards.

GET READY

- Take turns picking cards from the deck—the first player to pick a Brother card is the dealer.

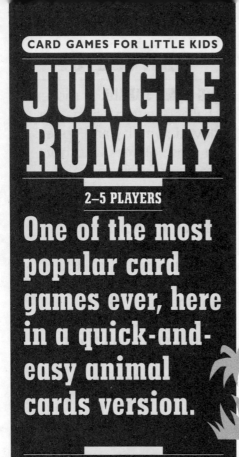

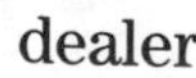

GET SET

DEALER: Hand out the cards, one at a time, picture-side-down. If you're playing with only two players, deal out eight cards each; for three, four, or five players, six cards each.

• Put the rest of the cards in a picture-side-down stack in the middle—this is the Jungle pile. Turn over the top card and put it picture-side-up beside the Jungle pile.

EVERYONE: Pick up your cards. Arrange them so that as many of them as possible form a family sequence or are matching family members. You are aiming to end up with all

your cards in one kind of three-card set or the other. (For two players, a set is four cards.) For instance, you might end up with three Brothers, and then also have the Sister, Mother, and Father of the Snake family. Within a family member set, the cards must be in sequence: for instance, Brother, Mother, Father does not count.

GO!

PLAYER ON DEALER'S LEFT: You may pick a new card from

the Jungle pile or the picture-side-up card next to it. Add the new card to your hand. Take one card out of your hand and discard it on top of the picture-side-up pile in the center. You can't discard the card you just picked.

● Play goes around to the left, with each player picking the top card from either the Jungle pile or the discard pile. The player then discards a card from her hand and her turn is finished.

● If the Jungle pile runs out, turn over the picture-side-up pile and start a new Jungle pile, making sure the top picture card stays picture-side-up.

● If all the cards in your hand are in sets, then you are ready to "leave the Jungle." You have to be able to do this on your turn, including picking a new card and putting out another card. Remember—you can't discard the same card you just picked. You must lay out all your cards so that the other players can see your sets.

WINNER: The first player to leave the Jungle is the winner.

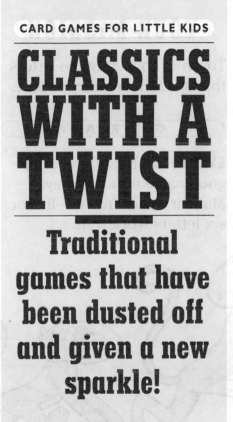

CLASSICS WITH A TWIST

Traditional games that have been dusted off and given a new sparkle!

From betting games (with candy and cookies instead of poker chips) to games better known abroad than in the United States, this final section is a collection of classic games tweaked to have a new, fresh appeal. Introducing more sophisticated elements of card play, such as trick-taking and trumps, these games place a bit more emphasis on skill than luck—but are still swift and easy when played with the animal card deck. Enjoy!

MONKEY SEE, MONKEY DO

4–6 PLAYERS

Imitation is the sincerest form of flattery—don't be the last little monkey to copy the crowd.

YOUR MISSION

To avoid collecting the letters that spell the monkey's name.

GET READY

EVERYONE: First think of one good name for a monkey. Make it a short name—five or six letters work well.

● Find some identical, unbreakable objects—like pennies or spoons or plastic counters. You need one less than the number of players.

● Each player gets a piece of paper and a pencil for scorekeeping.

● The tallest player is the dealer in this game.

DEALER: Pull from the deck an animal family for each player, so that if there are four of you, you have four animal families in the game. Put the rest of the families safely to one side—you won't need them for this game.

GET SET

EVERYONE: Sit in a circle. Put the collected identical objects in the center.

DEALER: Shuffle the cards so that the families are all mixed together. Then hand out the cards, one at a time and picture-side-down, to each player. Everyone should have four cards.

EVERYONE: Look at your cards. You are trying to collect a family. Choose one card you don't want and slide it picture-side-down to the neighbor on your right.

GO!

EVERYONE: Look at the card that's been passed to you. Decide whether to keep it or to pass it along. If you want to keep it, choose another card to pass. When everyone's ready, pass to the right again.

- When you've collected all the members of an animal family, take one of the objects from the center.

EVERYONE: When you see another player taking an object, that's your cue to copy her as quickly as you can. Join in the mad grab for the remaining objects!

- One player will not get to the objects in time. Write the

first letter of the monkey's name on that player's piece of paper.

- The player who lost the round gathers up all the objects and puts them in the center again, then deals out another round.

- If the same player loses again, he gets the next letter of the monkey's name.

- The first player to get all the letters of the monkey's name must dance around the room scratching and screeching just like a monkey.

WINNER: The last person remaining in the game (the one with the fewest monkey name letters) is the winner.

CHANGE-UP

- If you don't want to play with objects, you can use gestures. When a player has collected an animal family, instead of picking up an object from the center, she does a little monkey imitation—like peeling a banana or scratching under her arms or the top of her head. The last player to catch on and do the same gets a monkey name letter.

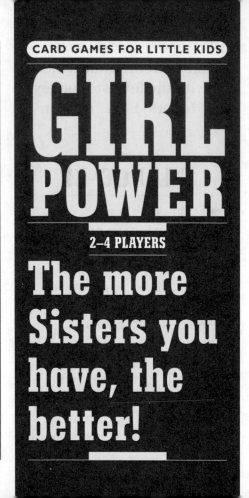

CARD GAMES FOR LITTLE KIDS

GIRL POWER

2–4 PLAYERS

The more Sisters you have, the better!

YOUR MISSION

To be the first player to earn 100 points.

GET READY

● The first player to pick a Sister from the deck is the dealer.

● Zebra cards are wild in this game.

● Pick a scorekeeper to keep track of everyone's scores. Get paper and a pencil to keep score—you'll be playing more than one round and the score will be tallied at the end of each round.

● Here's how to score: All cards (except for Zebra cards, which are wild) count for 5 points. At the end of each round, the winner (the player who gets rid of all her cards first) gets 5 points for each card in the losing players' hands. If a losing player has a Zebra, she gets 20 points

added to her score and the winner of that hand doesn't get any points for that card.

GET SET

DEALER: Hand out five cards to each player, one at a time and picture-side-down.

● Put the rest of the stack in the center. Turn over the top card and put it next to the stack.

EVERYONE: Look at your cards.

92

GO!

PLAYER TO DEALER'S LEFT: You go first. You must match the card in the center with a card from your hand by playing a card from the same family or a card that is the same family member. If you can't match the card in the center with a card from your hand, pick a card from the picture-side-down stack and add it to the cards in your hand.

● However, if the card in the center is a Sister, you *must* play a Sister. If you can't play a Sister, you must keep picking cards from the picture-side-down stack until you can. Or

you can play a Zebra card, including the Zebra Sister. If you do this, you can name what family or family member the next player must match, but you risk losing the 20-point Zebra bonus at the end of the round if you give away your Zebra card.

NEXT PLAYER: You must now match the card in the center. If it's a Sister, you are in the same position as the previous player; you must play a Sister or pick cards from the center until you can.

• Play moves clockwise with everyone trying to get rid of cards, avoid having to pick a lot of cards from the center, and keep hold of the Zebras until the last minute.

• If the center stack runs out, take the top card off the picture-side-up pile, put it back in place, shuffle the cards that were under it thoroughly, and use them to make a new center stack.

• The round ends when one player gets rid of all his cards: he is the winner of this round and gets 5 points for every card in the other players' hands. If play is blocked, the player with the fewest cards wins the round. However, this player must subtract from her total 1 point for every card left in her hand—and she cannot earn the 20-point Zebra bonus, if applicable.

• Play resumes with a fresh shuffle and deal.

WINNER: The first player to reach 100 points wins the game.

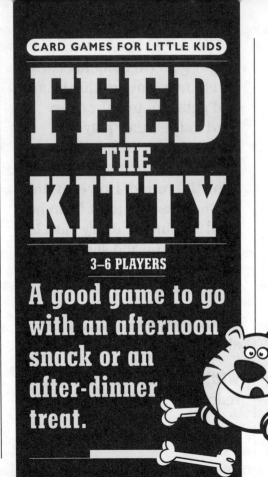

FEED THE KITTY

3–6 PLAYERS

A good game to go with an afternoon snack or an after-dinner treat.

YOUR MISSION

To win as many nibblies as possible.

GET READY

● Get a big bag of "nibblies": M&M's, Cheez Puffs, or raisins work well. Give everyone the same number of nibblies—about fifteen or twenty. Put a

bowl or dish in the center. This is the Kitty.

EVERYONE: Start picking cards from the deck. The first player to pick an Elephant card is the dealer.

GET SET

DEALER: Shuffle the cards. Hand out all the cards, one at a time and picture-side-down. It doesn't matter if some players have more cards than others.

EVERYONE: Pick up your cards and organize them in your hand by family member. If you have a complete family, show it to the other players and put it to one side. All the other players must feed a nibblie to the Kitty.

GO!

PLAYER ON DEALER'S LEFT: You must play a Brother card picture-side-up to the center. Say "Brother" as you play it. If you don't have a Brother, feed a nibblie to the Kitty. Your turn is over. Play goes around until a player can play a Brother to the center. Any player unable to play must feed a nibblie to the Kitty.

NEXT PLAYER: You have to put out the next family member in the sequence (Brother, Sister, Mother, Father) and say what it is—but it doesn't have to be from the same family. So if you're following Brother

Snake, you can play Sister Elephant, saying "Sister."

● When a Father is played, the next player must play a Brother.

● If you can't play the next family member in the sequence, then you must feed the Kitty a nibblie. Your turn is over.

● Play keeps going around with players either playing a card in the family sequence or feeding the Kitty.

WINNER: The first player to play all his cards is the winner. The other players must feed Kitty a nibblie for every card left in their hands. The winner wins all of the Kitty's nibblies.

EVERYONE: Eat up your nibblies before the next round. Then play again. Carry on until everyone is full.

CARD GAMES FOR LITTLE KIDS

JAWS

2–5 PLAYERS

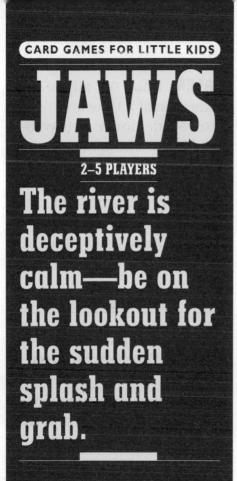

The river is deceptively calm—be on the lookout for the sudden splash and grab.

YOUR MISSION

To get rid of all your cards.

GET READY

- If there are three of you playing, remove one card from the deck—make sure it's not a member of the Crocodile family.

- Choose one player to be the scorekeeper and decide on a winning score—say, 50 points.

SCOREKEEPER: Set up a score sheet, with a column under each player's name or initial.

- The first player to pick a Crocodile from the deck is the dealer.

GET SET

DEALER: Hand out all the cards, one at a time and picture-side-down. Everyone should have the same number of cards.

EVERYONE: Pick up your cards and arrange them by family and in sequence—Brother, Sister, Mother, Father.

GO!

PLAYER ON DEALER'S LEFT: Choose a Brother card from a family for which you have the next card in the sequence. Play the Brother card and say what card it is, for instance,

"Brother Giraffe." (If you don't have a Brother card, your turn is over and play goes around to the next player who does.)

● Continue putting out cards from that family in sequence, as far as you can. If you can play the whole family, you must do so. The scorekeeper awards you 5 points for playing an entire family at one go. Then start a new family with another Brother. Once again, if you don't have a Brother, your turn is over.

NEXT PLAYER: You must either carry on the sequence the first player has begun or, if he played an entire family, start a new family with a Brother card

from your hand. If you are able to complete a family that a previous player or players started, the scorekeeper awards you 1 point.

● If you can't play the next card in the sequence, you must say so: "No Mother Zebra," for instance. Your turn is over, and the next player must try to continue the sequence.

- If you have Jaws—a.k.a. Sister Crocodile—you must play it when you can't continue a sequence. You get 2 points for playing the Jaws card.

NEXT PLAYER AFTER JAWS: You may either continue the Crocodile family sequence—this is your only chance to play all of your Crocodiles in a row—or continue the family sequence the Jaws card interrupted. If you can't do either, play goes around to the left until a player can do one or the other.

- Play continues until one player runs out of cards. The scorekeeper must then give that player 2 points for every Father left in the other players' hands and 1 point for any of the other players' other cards.

- The player who ran out of cards now collects all the cards, shuffles them well, and deals them out to start a new round.

WINNER: The winner is the first player to reach 50 points.

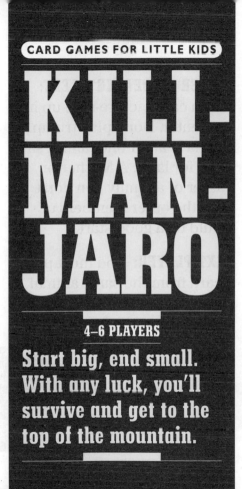

CARD GAMES FOR LITTLE KIDS

KILI-MAN-JARO

4–6 PLAYERS

Start big, end small. With any luck, you'll survive and get to the top of the mountain.

YOUR MISSION

To avoid being knocked off Kilimanjaro by winning tricks.

GET READY

● Take turns picking cards from the deck. The first player to pick a Tiger is the dealer.

GET SET

DEALER: Pick up the deck and ask the player on your left to pick a card. That card decides the trump family for the first hand. So if Sister Giraffe is picked, the Giraffe family is trump.

- Put the card back in the deck. Shuffle well. Hand out six cards, picture-side-down, to each player. Set the remaining cards to one side.

EVERYONE: Pick up your cards. Arrange your cards by family.

GO!

PLAYER ON DEALER'S LEFT: Play a card picture-side-up into the center. Don't play trump. If you have all of one family, save them for later. A Mother or Father of a family you don't have the other members of would be a good start.

NEXT PLAYER: You must play a card from the same animal family if you have one. Try to put out a card higher up in the family member sequence. If you don't have any of that family, then you can play a card from the trump family. If you are saving your trump card or don't have any, play a Brother or Sister card from another family.

• Play continues around to the left until everyone has played one card. Whoever played the highest card in the family or the highest card in the trump family wins the trick.

TRICK WINNER: Pick up your trick and put it in front of you. Start another round by playing another card to the center.

• When all six rounds have been played the first hand is over. If one player won all of the tricks, then she has won the game and you must start over. If someone didn't win any tricks, he is off Kilimanjaro and can't play any more hands.

• Whoever won the most tricks picks up all the cards, shuffles, and deals.

NEW DEALER: This time deal out only five cards for a hand of five rounds. Play the hand as before. For the next hand, the new dealer deals out only four cards, then three, then two, until in the final hand each remaining player has only one card. Whoever wins that hand wins the game.

WINNER: The last player still on Kilimanjaro is the winner.

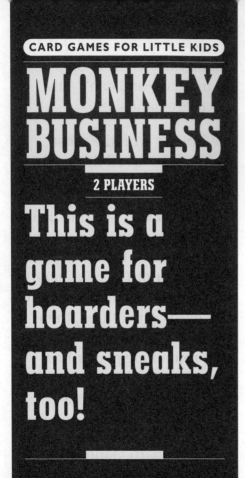

CARD GAMES FOR LITTLE KIDS

MONKEY BUSINESS

2 PLAYERS

This is a game for hoarders—and sneaks, too!

YOUR MISSION

To collect all the cards.

GET READY

- Take turns picking cards from the deck. The first person to pick a member of the Monkey family is the dealer.

GET SET

DEALER: Shuffle the cards. Hand out four cards, picture-side-down, to yourself, then four cards to the other player. Put four more cards picture-side-up in the middle. Set the rest of the cards aside.

BOTH PLAYERS: Pick up your cards and organize them by family member.

GO!

OTHER PLAYER: You go first. If you have a card in your hand that is the same family member as one of the cards in the center, you can "steal" the

matching card in the center. Put the matching card from your hand over the card in the center and put them both in a picture-side-up pile in front of you. This is your hoard.

- You must add cards to your hoard in exactly the order you took them.

- If you don't have a card that matches any of the four in the center, you must put a card from your hand picture-side-up in the center. Your turn is over.

- If you have two cards that match one card in the center, two Fathers, for instance, just play one of them at a time.

- You can steal as many cards from the center as you have matching cards in your hand.

DEALER: Play any cards you have that match the center cards, and steal accordingly, to add to your hoard.

- If you have a card that matches the picture-side-up card in the *other* player's hoard, you may steal her hoard and add it, picture-side-up, to your own.

BOTH PLAYERS: Take turns trying to match and steal and add to your hoard until both players have played the four cards they were dealt. If neither player has a match left in her hand, then both players put the cards they have left in the center.

DEALER: Hand out four more cards, picture-side-down, first to the other player, then to yourself. Don't put new cards in the center.

● On the final deal, whoever uses her last card to steal from the center also takes any remaining cards there.

WINNER: When there are no cards left to deal another hand of four each, the game is over. Count the number of cards in your hoard. The player with the most cards wins.

SNAKE PIT

4–5 PLAYERS

If you like taking chances—and can keep a cool head under pressure—this is a great game.

YOUR MISSION

To get rid of all your cards.

GET READY

- The shortest player gets to deal this game.

GET SET

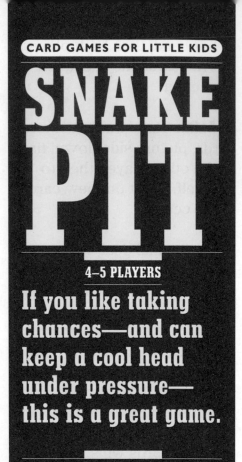

DEALER: Shuffle the cards. Deal each player ten cards

(or eight cards if you're playing with five players), one at a time and picture-side-down.

EVERYONE: Look at your cards. Arrange them by family member. Decide where the central discard pile (the Snake Pit) will go.

GO!

PLAYER ON DEALER'S RIGHT: You'll be the first to contribute cards picture-side-down into the Snake Pit. You must play one or more Brother cards if you have any—or you must pretend to play Brothers. Always say out loud what you're claiming to place on the pile: "Two Brothers," for instance.

- If you're faking it, as you play your cards into the Snake Pit—picture-side-down, of course—you'll need to fib when you say what the cards are (at least what you're pretending they are): "Three Brothers," for example.

Three "Brothers"

- You can also add to the Brothers you have with another card or two. So you can put out two cards, only one of which is a Brother, or you can put out three cards, none of which is a Brother. Remember to fib correctly.

NEXT PLAYER: You must play Sisters—or pretend to play Sisters. Add your cards to the Snake Pit, saying what they're supposed to be.

EVERYONE: Keep going around to the right, following the family sequence—when the Fathers have been played, go back to Brothers.

- Any player may decide another player is not telling the truth about the cards she says she is playing. If you're a bit skeptical, hiss like a snake—but only when she has just played the cards. Once the next player has put out his cards, it's too late.

- When you hiss, the other player must turn up the cards she just played. If you're right, she has to add all the cards in the Snake Pit to her hand. But if you're wrong and she was telling the truth, you have to add all of the Snake Pit cards to your hand.

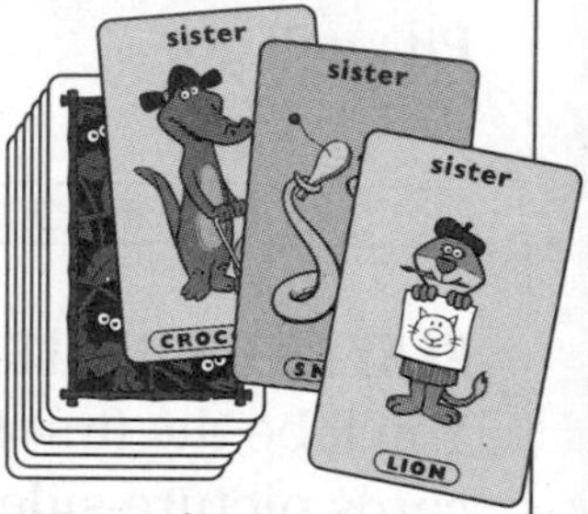

- Whichever player picked up the Snake Pit has to continue

by playing—or pretending to play—the next family member in the sequence.

- If two players hiss at the same time, the one with more at stake—that is, the player with *fewer* cards in his hand—is the challenger.

- Sometimes the Snake Pit has only one card in it—the card just played. So a "hissed" player may have to keep picking up the card she just played until the other players believe her.

WINNER: The first player to play all her cards into the Snake Pit is the winner.

CHANGE-UP

NEST OF VIPERS: Add a twist by giving players the option to either move up the family sequence *or* increase the number of cards.

- So if the previous player played two Brothers, the next player can play two Sisters, for example.

- Or if the previous player played two Brothers, the next player can play three or more Brothers.

EXTINCTION

3–5 PLAYERS

Outlasting the competition is vital. A game of patience and determination.

YOUR MISSION

To be the last player holding cards by winning tricks.

GET READY

- The oldest player deals the first hand.

● The youngest player decides trump for the game by picking a card at random from the deck. If he picks a Hippo, for instance, then the Hippo family is trump. This makes

them special. A card from the trump family beats all other cards. If two players play trump, then the trump card that is highest in the family sequencc wins the trick.

GET SET

DEALER: After shuffling the cards, hand them out, picture-side-down. Give each player as many cards as there are players. The remaining cards go in a picture-side-down stack in the middle.

EVERYONE: Pick up your cards and organize them by family.

GO!

PLAYER ON DEALER'S LEFT: Play a card, picture-side-up, into the center.

NEXT PLAYER: You must play a card from the same family if you have one in your hand.

If you can't, then play trump—in which case you're likely to win the trick—or a card from another family, preferably a Sister or Brother because they are least likely to win future tricks for you.

● When everyone has played a card, the round is over.

● Whoever played the highest card in the family sequence or the highest trump wins the trick.

TRICK WINNER: Put the finished trick neatly to one side. Pick a card from the middle and add it to your hand. Play any card you like into the center to start another round.

● Play goes around to the left as before: Everyone plays a card, and the trick winner gets to add another card from the stack to her hand.

● Any player who runs out of cards is extinct and must drop out of the game.

WINNER: The last player to run out of cards is the winner.

CARD GAMES FOR LITTLE KIDS

STAMPEDE

2–4 PLAYERS

This is a fast-paced game. To do well you need to be alert and a little crafty.

YOUR MISSION

To get rid of all your cards.

GET READY

- The tallest player gets to deal this game.

GET SET

DEALER: Shuffle the cards. Hand them out, one card at a time, picture-side-down. It doesn't matter if some players have more cards than others.

EVERYONE: Don't look at your cards. Put them picture-side-down in a pile in front of you.

GO!

PLAYER ON DEALER'S LEFT: Turn over your top card. If it's a Brother, put it in the middle and turn over another card. All Brothers are put in the middle. If it's a Sister from the same family, put it on top of the Brother. If it's not a Brother,

put it picture-side-up right next to your stack of cards to end your turn.

NEXT PLAYER: Turn over a card.

- If it's the Sister of the same family as the Brother in the center, put it on top of the Brother. Cards that go in the center must be the same family, in sequence.

● If it's not the Sister of that same family, check to see whether it can go on top of the first player's picture-side-up

card stack. For instance, if her picture-side-up card was the Mother Crocodile, you could cover it with any Father—it doesn't need to be from the same family as long as it's next highest in the sequence: Brother, Sister, Mother, Father.

● Turn over another card; if you can't play it, then it starts your own picture-side-up pile. (If you couldn't play your first card, then it starts your own picture-side-up pile.)

● Play goes around to the right. A turn lasts as long as the player is able to play turned-up cards to either the center (a new Brother or the next member in the family sequence) or any other player's picture-side-up piles (any family, in sequence). Each turn ends with a player adding a card to his own picture-side-up pile.

● If you run out of cards in your picture-side-down pile in the middle of a turn, turn over your picture-side-up pile and continue. If you've played your final card onto your picture-side-up pile, wait until your next turn to turn that pile over—other players may want to put cards on top of the one you just played.

WINNER: The first person to get rid of all his cards by placing them in the middle or on other people's piles is the winner.

CARD GAMES FOR LITTLE KIDS

THE TIGER CHASES ITS TAIL

4–6 PLAYERS

A game of going around in circles—fun, frustrating, and fast-moving all at the same time. Extra fun for hungry kids!

YOUR MISSION

To win lots of cookies.

GET READY

- Round up a package or two of cookies—you'll need at least three cookies per player to begin.

EVERYONE: Sit in a circle. Take turns picking cards from the deck. The first player to pick a card from the Tiger family gets to be the dealer.

GET SET

DEALER: Give each player three cookies. Shuffle the cards and give each player one card, picture-side-down.

EVERYONE: Peek at your card without picking it up.

GO!

PLAYER ON DEALER'S LEFT: If your card is a parent—a Father or Mother card—you should keep it. Say "I'm keeping it."

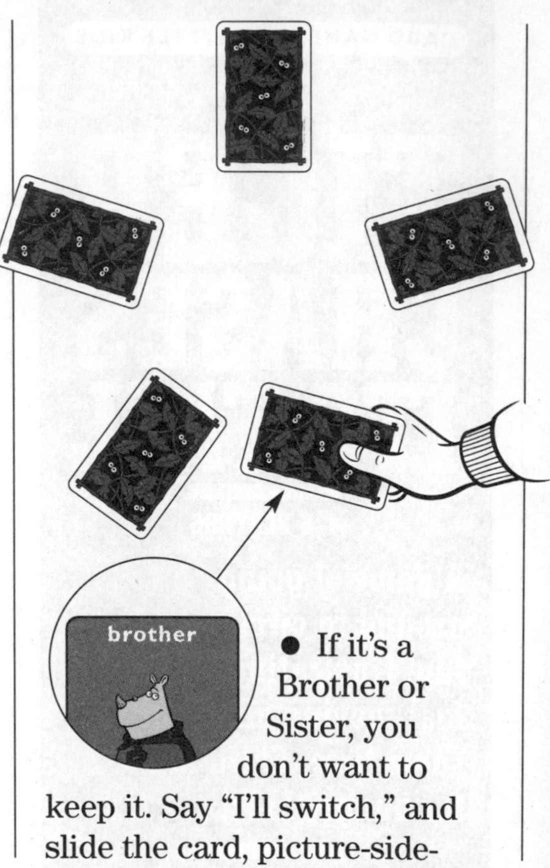

- If it's a Brother or Sister, you don't want to keep it. Say "I'll switch," and slide the card, picture-side-down, to the player on your left.

● Everyone will be trying to get rid of any Brother cards, so the Brother cards end up moving around the circle, like a Tiger chasing its tail.

PLAYER ON LEFT: You must accept the switch—unless the card you have in front of you is a Father. If that is the case, you show your Father card to the other players and you get to keep it. The first player then has to switch with the person sitting to *your* left.

NEXT PLAYER: After you've received your new card, peek at it. Decide whether to keep your new card or switch with the player sitting to your left.

● Play continues around the circle until it gets back to the dealer.

DEALER: You have the last turn in the round. You can't switch with anyone, but if you don't like your card, you may bury it in the deck and pick a new card from the top. If the new card is a Father, you automatically lose the round and a cookie. If you don't trade in your card, or if your new card isn't a Father, just turn your card picture-side-up.

EVERYONE: When the dealer signifies the round has ended

by turning over her card, you must all turn over your cards. Whoever has a Brother card loses and must put a cookie in the middle.

- If there aren't any Brothers, then whoever has the lowest card must put a cookie in the middle.

- If everyone has the same card—Mothers, for instance—then everyone must put a cookie in the middle.

- If you have lost all three of your cookies, you are out of the game.

PLAYER TO LEFT OF LAST ROUND'S DEALER: Round up all the old cards and put them at the bottom of the deck. Deal a new round—one card to each player, picture-side-down—from the top of the deck.

WINNER: The last player to have a cookie left is the winner and gets to share all the cookies in the middle with the other players.

KING OF THE JUNGLE

2–8 PLAYERS

Get wily—the trickier your thinking, the better you'll do. Just remember who's boss.

YOUR MISSION

To win lots of tricks.

GET READY

● No creature is sneakier than the Snake—so whoever picks a Snake first is dealer in this game.

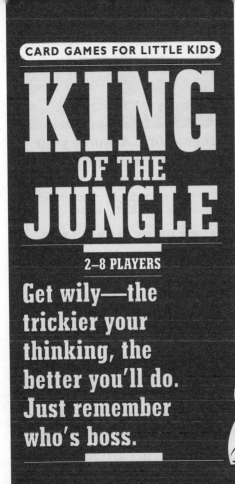

124

GET SET

DEALER: If you have two, four, five, or eight players, you can use the entire deck. If you have three or six players, remove one family—not the Lions. If you have seven players, remove one family—not the Lions—plus one additional card. Shuffle the cards. Hand out all the cards, one at a time and picture-side-down.

EVERYONE: Pick up your cards. Lions are wild in this game—that means any Lion card is higher than a card from any of the other families, so Sister Lion is higher than

Father Zebra. Arrange your cards with families together.

GO!

PLAYER ON DEALER'S LEFT: Play your highest card picture-side-up into the center—that is, play a Father card from any family—except Lions—if you have one.

NEXT PLAYER: You must play a card from the same family if you can. So if the first player put out a Giraffe, you must play a Giraffe card if you have

one. If you can, play a higher card in the sequence: If the first player put out a Mother Giraffe, for instance, and you have the Father Giraffe, then play it. If you don't have any of the same family, you can play a Lion card if you like, although you may want to save your Lion for later. If you don't have any cards from the same family or any Lions, play a Brother or Sister from some other family.

- Keep playing, going around clockwise, playing the same family if you can. When everyone has had a turn, the round is finished. Whoever played the highest card in the original family wins the trick. If Lions have been played, whoever played the higher Lion wins.

TRICK WINNER: Pick up the trick and put it neatly picture-side-down in front of you. Start another round by playing the highest card you have.

WINNER: When all the cards have been played, the game is over. The player with the most tricks is the winner.

INDEX